Other World

AF623593

Bree Elizabeth Powers

BookLeaf Publishing

Presentation by *BookLeaf Publishing*

Web: www.bookleafpub.com

E-mail: info@bookleafpub.com

ISBN: 9789357212571

First edition 2023

Dedicated to the ghost in my house.

PREFACE

Most of the entries in this book are descriptions of dreams or make-believe adventures. The're the stories I make up in my head in the middle of the night when I can't sleep or age-old memories so rudely invading my thoughts. Stories of murders and ghosts and heroes and opinions, legends, and myths, and all the curious, mysterious, beautiful things in the world.
Things bigger than we'll ever understand - otherworldly wonders and ideas and inventions, contraptions and traps, and life and death.
And I've written all about it.

I've learned to step away from public opinion and see something for the beauty of it. To transform something into an idea or concept that feels real and relatable and right.
And this is the outcome of my twisted vision. This is the end then.

Adam and Eve

In the beginning
There was Adam and Eve
But the end of the world
Will be just
You and me.

This is how you save me

I had a dream
I was standing in a field
With nothing around me
I don't know what it means but
In my dream
A crow flew up
And circled around me
So wild and so free
Then a fire started
And I couldn't see it
But I could hear and feel it burning me
So, I screamed
But no one heard me
And I was in the sun
With no shade or trees
So, I might have been hallucinating
But I'd deny any accusations that I was going crazy
And I was dying of heat
And ironically the sun came down and saved me
And she took my hand
And told me
"You need to save these people you meet"
And she said not to let their differences blind me
And I fell asleep

In my dream.
And when I woke up
It was night
And the moon was high above me
Making faces at me
And the image is blurry
But I remember the chair
And the desk
At which I was sitting
Still in the field
I heard someone start crying
And a child said
"You need to help me"
And I said
"How?"
And then I was somewhere else.

I was looking through the eyes
Of a scared little child
And all I could hear was screaming
And the actions weren't mind
But the arm on me moved
And some folk song started playing
And I recognized the story
As one that I would tell
And I blinked
And I was back in the field.

The sun was once again above me
A little child standing in front of me
With a pen and a paper
Saying

"This is how you save me."

Close my eyes

If I close my eyes
Even just to blink
All I see is you
You in everything
It's a comfortable thought
If you'd stop and think
But you slammed the brakes
Slammed right into me

Cause when you close your eyes
All you see is me

Even just to cry
Me in everything
And it keeps you in line
In the out-of-place
Cause even closing your eyes
Is a dangerous game.

And the demons haunting you
Look just like me
And they're trying to show you things
In the out-of-reach
And they whisper in your ear
All the lovely things

But they're trying to tell you
What they never told me

Cause the friends I used to have
End up enemies
And they're trying to take you places
That are make-believe
But I'm warning you
I'm telling you
Never trust thieves
But you said why should I trust you
When you never trust me?

If I close my eyes
Even just to sleep
Never told me why
You in everything
Say a sacred prayer
Tell a little lie
Even just to blink
I can't close my eyes

Rivers streaming down my cheeks like it's a race
Tears are pouring to my lips and they're salty to taste
And the room is on fire, hot with all my shame
Cause even closing your eyes is a dangerous game

And there are 8 billion persons in a tiny space
And it almost makes you wonder if they'd kill to escape
But my blood on your knife is really all it takes,
Cause even closing your eyes,
You still see my face.

This is what dying feels like

So, this is what dying feels like?
A punch in the face?
Your words hurt me more than the pain that your hands could make.
So, this is the end of a life?
The end of a day.
Tomorrow, I'll wake up and be fine
But right now,
Tell everyone I'm dead and I died.

This is hot
Then freezing cold
This is when never growing up
Starts getting old.
This is the air
Escaping from my lungs
And my body goes numb
This is the fault of my own
For not listening
When they told me to run

Now I paint with the blood.

I tell stories of ghosts
And of women who have too much fun.

And I looked in the mirror
And realized I crave the sun.
I was tied in my lies for so long
Now I'm coming undone.
But the freedom I found
Wasn't worth all the time that I lost.
There's a penny for your thoughts.

So, this is what dying feels like?
Alone in the dark?
I tried for so long
To build walls
To protect my heart
So, this the end of my life?
Death of a mastermind?
But the fault is mine
This is what dying feels like.

Tis the season

Summer is over
And you know
That it will be back
The wind in my hair
Is getting colder
Soon it will snow
And cover my tracks

The ice on the ground
Won't allow
My tiptoeing around
Lamp-lit corners
I saw you last night
Laughing harder than ever
Glad that you're happy
And sad that it's over
You know what they say
"… and that's why you should pray"
Why learn to love God
When he's so easy to blame?

Like…
What is the point of my existence?
What does Santa do when it's not Christmas?
Some middle-class divorcee business?

You know I hate winter
But God I love Christmas
Carolers singing
"Tis the season"
But at least last year
I had a reason
Now memories swing in
Got me acting so vicious
You know I hate winter
But God I love Christmas.

Last Words

I'm fragile
Like glass
Dropping on grass
Delicate
But I'll make it
Maybe next time
I'll be sitting in class
And I'll have the urge to say
What needs to be said
All the thoughts in my head
Monsters under my bed
Follow me into the basement
I'll scream and I'll say,
"What lives dies today"
And my last words will make me famous

And we can play ISpy the irony of that
Isn't it kind of funny?
The irony of that?

I'm running like water
Into the wonders
Of Other Worlds
Where I haven't been
The stars make me smaller

Your song made me stronger
I learned to protect myself
From politics, opinions, and men

And I can say
What needs to be said
All the thoughts in my head
And the monsters are friends
And yeah, I know you hate it
So, you'll stomp on my grave
Try to put me to shame
But my last words have made me famous.

Seven

I remember being seven
On the swings all of the time
My bruised knees would swing to heaven
And back to earth in the blink of an eye
My mystical land life below me
My mother calling me for lunch
I remember being seven
and never wanting to grow up

Hurt feelings
And a couple boys later
I remember being seven
I remember all the anger
Sweet bliss of mine remembers
While my soul one day forgot
I remember being seven
I remember it all

Somehow in the darkness
Tucked under my blanket
I'm still there
I dream about it
Seven
I still dream about it

"She's innocent until she's not"
Well, I turned eight and all forgot
What magic lies in seven
Being seven
I remember
Being seven.

Labyrinth

My mind is a labyrinth
A sky to get lost in
I think of dying
Not as a bad thing
But as a blessing
If you think about it hard enough
You can feel the earth spinning
You get dizzy
and have to sit down
But it's worth it for the second
when your body enters an Other World
and it's like you're flying.
Did you see Halley's Comet
more than once?
Did you live the life you wanted?
My mind is a labyrinth
I'm constantly getting lost in.

My mind is my refuge
from everything real and right and true
Christmas day
"New year, new you"
What you put in the world
comes back to you
And if you think about it hard enough

there are people in the world
who must hate the people like you
And that’s so sad to me
To live your life pointing fingers
And blaming
Like you’ve got nothing better to do

My mind is a labyrinth
A sky to get lost in
Everything good must have gotten lost
Because the world that we live in
is violent and dangerous
Where everything good
comes with a cost
My mind is a labyrinth
Take a dive off a cliff
And settle in…

sun in my eyes

When I die
I want the sun in my eyes
Somewhere in the mountains
Where no one else ever is
Maybe I'll trip
And fall off a cliff
And collide with the dirt
Maybe it'd hurt
I have only one request
And you'll try your best
So, when I die
I have the sun in my eyes
So I can't see
The beautiful world I'm leaving
Maybe it'd start raining
And wash away my sins and mistakes
So I'm ready for heaven
Maybe they won't know I'm dead
Until I'm gone
The trees conceal what's going on
Maybe my legacy will carry on
For generations and generations
Like some kind of folk song
But when I die
I want the sun in my eyes…

Ellipsis

You couldn't save me
Even if you tried
I'm too far gone
To know day from night
The woman who raised me
Must have done something right
But I couldn't tell you what that is

Now I'm standing at the edge of a cliff
Smiling at the water like if I jumped
This all would end
Pretending that you might give a shit
If I died
Like you might even cry
If I ended my life
Throw my body in the street
Leave my life incomplete
Like some kind of ellipsis

No one knows how far I've come except for me
That's what it feels like at least
My body and mind are in two different stages of existing
It's so confusing
But the woman who raised me

Has helped me get through it
Everything around me is moving in slow motion
I bet she didn't know that
Terrified of the ocean
Which is funny cause I grew up in the water
I guess people change
I guess I'm your proof then

Now I'm standing on some old broken ship
Smiling at my feet
Like I'm asking where they'll take me
Everyone knows I'm not a kid
So, I wish they'd stop treating me like it
Before I walk the plank
And walk into some kind of ellipsis

"Dot dot dot"
Was my thought
When I ran away from home
Like "where will I go?"
And the woman who raised me
Didn't know

…

Throw my body in the street.
Hide my genius in the trees.
Let me know if you would rather, I die young or forever live.

Win the war or face defeat.
Leave my life incomplete.
Let me know if you would rather, I fall into an ellipsis.

I didn't know what else to say...

You brought me to God
And you taught me to pray
You gave me the world
And then took it away
Said the sky was blue
So, you painted it gray
I don't know what to say
Now I'm getting older
Things are getting worse
My mind is a prison
I live with the shame and the trauma and hurt
I don't know how to help myself
I can barely breathe
I guess if its true what you say
And I'm really a bitch
Then I'm the bitch that you made
Can't you take that away?
Then my goal in life is to be happy someday
As somebody else
So, I created a name
And if I need to hide
I'll dye my hair
And start calling myself "Elizabeth Mae"
My plan B is called "The great escape"

Yet I’m terrified
That this family will haunt me someday
And I’m scared you’ll abandon me
As soon as I’m of age
And sure, I’m no saint
I’ve made countless mistakes
When they ask me my name
I don’t know what to say
Cause “Powers” is a name I don’t own
Even to this day
I’m sorry if this hurts
But I didn’t know what else to say
You brought me to God
And in the end
It’s Him that I blame
I didn't know what else to say...

I speak for the Ghosts

I speak for the Ghosts
Who have something to say
I throw you across the room
And punch you in the face
And they channel their anger through me
And that's why I'm so angry
As if I had to explain
I speak for the kids who
Life wasn't fair too
I'm friends with the ghost in my house
'Cause I dared to
Introduce myself and say
"My home is your home"
You know how this goes
I speak for the ghosts

we're all going to die

The sand on the beach is the only proof that I
was there
Lost in the sky and the sea
My mind was anywhere but here
Somebody spoke too soon as my footsteps
echoed through the stairwell
"Oh well"
They said
"Speak of the Devil and behold she appears "

"You're treading on thin ice" is a favorite saying
of mine
Because it also happens to be my favorite
pastime
I seem to enjoy crossing every line
And then lying
And denying that I committed such crimes

You know better than I do
Let's leave it at that
My sky is filled with despair
As I stare
And watch the Universe get mad
I could point fingers
But really, what's the point?

We're all going to die anyways
And float away into some bleak empty void

My self-esteem fell like snow falling in October
So now, whatever I had left of it is gone
As I sit on my bed, in my head
There's a war going on
1 against 2
Me vs. the Liar and the Fraud
I never seem to win…

"Karma's a real bitch"
Would be the first thing out of my mouth in my end-of-the-world speech
And I'd turn and walk away until all they could see was my middle finger in the sky
Because who even cares if we're all going to die?

I got the gift of attitude
So, what do I do except give it to you?
No one knows why there are stars in the sky
But at least we all know of our perfect demise
We're all going to die :)

Outrageous

That’s outrageous
Saying I’m dangerous
Like I’m acting so heinous
It’s not like I’m manic
You’re just faithless
Stupid emotions.

That’s outrageous
Saying I’m courageous
Put me out of business
I’m running out on Christmas
I don’t call them dreams
They’re my twisted visions
You said
“That’s outrageous”

…

GLORYANDHELL

"The Earth is full. Go somewhere else."
I won't admit that I need help
And I'm bad with words
But I can write a story of
Glory and Hell
And then never let it be seen by someone else.

I pick my nails
I pull my hair out
Trust me,
I'm an even bigger disappointment to myself
I get sick from the worry
Of Glory and Hell
So, I write the songs
To get the rage out

The sky is my blanket,
It keeps me warm.
With God as my witness,
I'm going to war.
My words are my weapons,
You're in for a storm.
Look in the mirror,
I'm in for a storm.

I've been destined for
Glory and Hell
Since before I was born.

The moon is mine
He said so himself
And then turned me in
And took his wealth
It's a horrible story of
Glory and Hell
So, why would I tell it to somebody else?

Nobody knows
Where anyone goes
When somebody dies
The sweet wind whispers
"Nobody dies if they haven't first lived"
It's a common phrase among us masterminds
And geniuses
Either name fits...

aurora borealis green

Tide washed in
All my progress
Swept away to the sea
There's no proof
That loving you
Will turn out bad for me
I shout and scream
And say things I won't ever ever mean
There's something in the blue
Hiding in the aurora borealis green
Saw you on the tv screen
And said "that's what I'll be"
Inspiration to the generation
Hiding behind me
I'll take these sticks and stones
And line them up along the creak
I'll grow and I'll get old
And I'll tell stories of my dreams
In the aurora borealis green
Isn't it so pretty…
The way that I think?
You look at me and don't think
That I'm like some ship lost at sea
My mind is my greatest enemy
Tide washed in

All the monsters
Came and greeted me
That's the story
Of hell and glory
At the aurora borealis green
You said "don't make a scene"
Took one look at my bruised knees
And said
"There's no proof that loving you will be enough for me"
That's what I remember when they complement your ring…
But I see it in my dreams…
The aurora borealis green

Golden Affair

I ran outside
for a breath of air.
I saw you standing there
just like a ghost.
Follow me to the garden where
our secret can remain a golden love affair
If nobody sees it than nobody knows
but your integrity is holding a gun to its head
Tell them you're working
and to leave you alone
Then drive across town to join her in bed
The soundtrack to your life then is "Karma's
going to get you"
Right when you least expect it.
And paint your golden affair black and blue.

monster trucks

I'm standing in the window
Like a dress on display
You say that only I know
What keeps you awake

I've been wearing ruby red
To match my lips that you stained
I'm hiding in the mountains when I'm older
Just so I can get away
From the monster I made
I know who they love
They don't love me
They love Elizabeth Mae
And who do I think I am
to get to take that away?
I'm driving monster trucks off the road
and out of this state
It isn't love
It isn't hate

I'm running to the safe house
You said would be safe
I'm one with the earth, the sea, and the rain
I've been playing hide and seek
To find the time when your love was claimed

I’m so ashamed…
Of the monster I made…

I know who they want
They don’t want me
They want Elizabeth Mae
And who am I to have to tell them
she’s more than a name?
I’m crashing monster trucks
driving them too fast on the highway
It isn’t Karma
It’s fate
Take my monster trucks away.

Couldn't we talk?

Couldn’t we talk?
Couldn’t I meet you before you get caught?
Slip through the door before it gets locked?
Couldn’t you treat me like I’m more than the rust on your door?
Instead of walking all over me like the creak in the floor?
Couldn’t we talk?
Couldn’t you meet me around 10 o’clock?
Sneak out or break out
Just love let's unpause
Couldn’t we talk?
The women who wear high heels left tracks in the snow
Couldn’t we meet so I could let you know?
The answer is easy unless it’s just no.
You believe in God, and I believe in ghosts
What’s the difference?
No one knows
But you could and I could
If we could just talk.
Instead of running around while our elders scream “stop”
Couldn’t we talk?
Three words every two steps on the sidewalk?

Found me then lost me
I’m still kind of lost
Couldn’t we talk?

Starless Sea

I don’t dream of flying or falling
Or losing my mind.
Or walking the tightrope or fighting with Time.
My dreams don’t consist of finding a true love
But you found me last night.
I was hiding away from human civilization
One some star that I loved, so I claimed.
My mind was a ghost town,
A cold empty basement
My mind is the storm in the clouds while it
rains.

My mind is an island on a serene, starless sea
My words are a ship sailing to me.
They come like a pattern
Like the waves or a breeze
And they fit in the puzzle like some missing
piece.

I don’t dream of fame or of fortune
Or walking the plank.
Or walking on water or messing with Fate.
My dreams don’t include loving or losing you
But it still seems to happen every day.
I was hiding away from the harsh awful truth

Dancing across a constellation I found.
My mind was a wasteland
Littered with amazement
My mind was the round of applause as I bowed.

My mind is an island on a serene, starless sea.
Your words are the cannon balls flying at me.
They come filled with hatred.
Well, my blood is my ink.
And the Others will drown in my silent, starless sea.

the end of the story...

So, I learned…
Of Adam and Eve
It didn't really help me
There's only one way to help me
This Is How You Save Me.
When I Close my eyes
It all comes back to me
The dying sensation
I feel every night
I can tell you exactly what dying feels like.
"Tis the season" talks of Christmastime
My Seven Last words were a trying time…
I talk of Labyrinths and of the sun in my eyes
Because my sweet mind insists
I learned of new words such as Ellipsis
And now that I use them every day
I'll never know what else to say…
"I speak for the ghosts" was a dream my mind made
And we're all going to die is our glorious Fate
I said that's Outrageous.
And my writing is me outside of my shell
So, I told you the story of GLORYANDHELL
And now that I've retold all of my dreams

I’ll tell you my favorite is the aurora borealis
green
It’s me in the air
My Golden Affair
It’s me driving monster trucks out of the state
I promise it’s me
And we couldn’t just talk
We had to scream
So, I left you to drown in my serene, Starless
Sea
But I guess that’s the end of this story…

www.ingramcontent.com/pod-product-compliance
Lightning Source LLC
Chambersburg PA
CBHW051742130826
49812CB00033B/970
* 9 7 8 9 3 5 7 2 1 2 5 7 1 *